Light and Dark

Revised and Updated

Angela Royston

Heinemann Library
Chicago, Illinois

© 2002, 2008 Heinemann Library
a division of Pearson Inc.
Chicago, Illinois

Customer Service 888-454-2279
Visit our website at www.heinemannlibrary.com

Editorial: Diyan Leake
Design: Joanna Hinton-Malivoire
Picture research: Melissa Allison and Mica Brancic
Production: Duncan Gilbert

Originated by Chroma Graphics (Overseas) Pte Ltd
Printed and bound in China by South China Printing Co. Ltd
12 11 10 09 08
10 9 8 7 6 5 4 3 2 1

Library of Congress Cataloging-in-Publication Data
Royston, Angela.
  Light and dark. / Angela Royston– New ed. –

  ISBN 13: 978-1-4329-1435-6 (HC)   ISBN 13: 978-1-4329-1457-8 (Pbk)
  ISBN 10: 1-4329-1435-9 (HC)   ISBN 10: 1-4329-1457-X (Pbk)
  Light – Juvenile literature. 2. Shades and shadows--Juvenile
literature.[1. Light. 2. Shadows.] I. Title
  QC360 .R69 2001
  535--dc21
                    00-012871

Acknowledgements
The publishers would like to thank the following for permission to reproduce photographs: © Corbis pp. **6, 26** (Pablo Corral); © Comstock p. **21**; © Ecoscene p. **25** (Nick Hawkes); © istockphoto.com p. **11** (Alex Slobodkin); © Jim McDonald p. **13**; © Kevin Fleming p. **20**; © Masterfile p. **10** (Bill Frymire); © Retina p. **16**; © Robert Harding pp. **5, 7**; © Science Photo Library p. **24** (Bruce Mackie); © Still Pictures p. **27** (Jeri Gleiter); © Trevor Clifford pp. **4, 9, 12, 14, 15, 17, 18, 19, 22, 23, 28, 29**; © Trip p. **8** (H. Rogers).

Cover photograph reproduced with permission of © Photolibrary/Corbis.

The publishers would like to thank Jon Bliss for his assistance in the preparation of this book.

Every effort has been made to contact copyright holders of any material reproduced in this book. Any omissions will be rectified in subsequent printings if notice is given to the publishers.

Contents

Any words appearing in the text in bold, **like this**, are explained in the glossary.

What Is Light?

Light allows us to see things. Light bounces off things and passes into our eyes.

This boy can see the plant because light is bouncing off it and into his eyes.

headlights

You can see more in bright light than in **dim** light. At night, drivers use lights to see the road and other traffic. How many car **headlights** can you see? (Answer on page 31.)

Daylight

It is easy to see during the day. The Sun is the **source** of daylight. The Sun's light is bright, so we can see clearly.

Sunlight is so strong it can **damage** your eyes. Never look directly at the Sun. Wear sunglasses in bright sunlight to **protect** your eyes.

Darkness

It is dark at night because the Sun is hidden by the Earth. Some light comes from the stars. The Moon **reflects** some light from the Sun. When there is no light, you cannot see anything.

You can use a box to see what it is like
to have no light at all. Keep the box
completely closed except for a small hole.
If you look through the hole, it will be too
dark inside the box to see anything.

Electric Lights

Electricity can make **sources** of light. At night we switch on lights so that we can see. Lightbulbs make a bright light.

Computers use electricity to light up the screen. Televisions also have screens that are lit by electricity.

More Lights

When something burns, it makes light.
Candles and paraffin lamps burn slowly,
so they can make light for a long time.

paraffin lamp

Fireworks make light too. The light is very bright, but it only lasts for a few seconds. Fireworks are easiest to see at night.

Comparing Lights

Some lights are brighter than others. The lamp in the picture is brighter than the lights on the tree, but **dimmer** than the spotlight. The spotlight is the brightest light.

spotlight

These flashlights are all shining. The smallest flashlight is dimmer than the middle flashlight. Which one is the brightest? (Answer on page 31.)

Reflected Light

This coat has strips and patches that **gleam** brightly at night. They gleam when light hits them and bounces off. This light is **reflected** light.

taps

Shiny things reflect more light than **dull** ones. The taps in the picture reflect more light than the sponge, the towel, and the toy animals.

Mirrors

You can see yourself in a mirror because it **reflects** the light from your face straight back to you. Mirrors can also be used to make a light brighter.

The bulb in a flashlight makes some light. The shiny surface behind the bulb reflects the light. The reflected light makes the flashlight light brighter.

Transparent Objects

Some **materials** are **transparent**. This means that you can see through them. Clear glass is transparent, so it is a good material to use for windows.

Plastic can be transparent, too. You
can see what is in a clear plastic bottle
because most of the light passes through
the bottle. A **translucent** bottle only lets
a small amount of light through.

Objects that Block Light

Some objects let no light pass through them. They are called **opaque**. If you hold a book in front of a light, you will no longer see the light.

This girl is using the door to play "Peek-a-Boo" with the child. The child cannot see through the door because it is opaque.

Light and Shade

We get most of our light from the Sun. When something gets in the way of the sunlight, it makes a shadow called a shade.

Clouds also make shadows on the
ground. You can still see when it is cloudy
because there is so much **reflected** light
all around you.

Shadows

When an object blocks light, it makes a dark shadow. When people stand in a sunny spot, their body blocks the light. It makes a shadow.

Light rays cannot pass through solid objects. When the Sun is low in the sky, objects on the ground make long shadows.

Shadow Shapes

Light always travels in straight lines. The light is blocked where there is an object. A shadow may be wider or longer than the object itself if the light is not close up to it.

The shadow of the vase is the same shape as the vase itself, but it is bigger.

If the object that is blocking light moves, the shadow will move. This shadow looks like a bird. If the hands move, the shadow will look like a flying bird.

Glossary

damage hurt or injure

dim not bright

dull not shiny

electricity power or force that can make something work

gleam shine

headlight large light at the front of a car, bus, truck, or other vehicle

material what something is made of

opaque lets no light through it

protect look after

reflect bounce back

source place that light come from

translucent lets some of the light through it

transparent lets all of the light through it

Answers

Page 5—There are eight car headlights in the photo.

Page 15—The biggest flashlight, the one on the left, is the brightest.

More Books to Read

Cooper, Christopher. *Light: From Sun to Bulbs*. Chicago: Heinemann Library, 2004.

Sadler, Wendy. *Electricity: Turn it On!*. Chicago: Raintree, 2006.

Sadler, Wendy. *Light: Look Out!*. Chicago: Raintree, 2006.

Index